AF585266

ENGINEERING MARVELS OF AUSTRALIA

Australia's Communications Structures

Alison Hideki

Redback Publishing
PO Box 357 Frenchs Forest NSW 2086
Australia

www.redbackpublishing.com.au
orders@redbackpublishing.com.au

978-1-925630-75-6

Author: Alison Hideki
Editor: Michael Anderson
Proofing: Marianne Lindsell
Designer: Redback Publishing

Original illustrations © Redback Publishing 2018
Originated by Redback Publishing

Printed and bound in Malaysia

Acknowledgements
Abbreviations: l—left, r—right, b—bottom, t—top, c—centre, m—middle
We would like to thank the following for permission to reproduce photographs: (Images © shutterstock) p8m - State library VIC, Construction of the Overland Telegraph 1871, Samuel Calvert, p9b - National Library Australia, Camp of the Overland Telegraph Line workers at Roper River, Northern Territory, approximately 1870, Samuel Sweet - PIC Box PIC/15724 #PIC/15724/5, p10b - State Library VIC, Planting of the first post of the overland telegraph 1870, Samuel Calvert, p11m - National Library Australia, Workers on the Overland Telegraph Line 1870, Samuel Sweet - PIC Box PIC/15724 #PIC/15724/1, p16t - Z22 via Wikimedia commons, p16b - www.atlantic-cable.com, Section of 1865 cable core recovered in 1866, p18b - State library VIC, Unidentified steamship 1920, Allan C Green c1900 - c1954, p19t - The institution of engineering and technology, Bow-sheevs and the Grapnel-hook, p22b - State Library VIC, Laying telephone wires from Darwin to Alice Springs 1944, Argus, p23b - State library VIC, Wills St. Exchange, trunk lines, 1910, p24t - State library Queensland, Sir John Forrest, neg 24.13,145.65, p26t - NASA via Wikimedia commons, p28t - Parkes, CSIRO via Wikimedia commons, p28m - Parkes Radio Telescope, CSIRO via Wikimedia commons, p29m - Five antennas at Narrabri, CSIRO via Wikimedia commons, p30m - Parkes telescope CSIRO via Wikimedia commons

A catalogue record for this book is available from the National Library of Australia

Contents

Communicating with the World 4

The Overland Telegraph 6

- The Plan 8
- Construction 10
- The End 12

The Bass Strait Submarine Cable 14

- Construction 16
- Laying the Cable 18
- The End of Cables 20

Building the Telephone Network 22

- One of the World's Best 24

The Parkes Radio Telescope 26

- Building the Dish 28

Cables and Signals Tourism 30

Glossary 31

Index 32

Find Out More 32

Communicating with the World

Today we have several devices and systems that enable us to communicate with people all over the world. With mobile phones, the internet and television, we can send and receive signals as pictures, sounds and text. Communications we take for granted today would hardly have been dreamt of 100 years ago. But communications within Australia and between Australia and other parts of the world have been important ever since Europeans arrived in Australia. Designing and building structures and systems for communications has involved inventors, designers and engineers continually improving and building on their achievements.

AMAZING FEATS

Many feats of engineering are remembered for their originality, their beauty and for the difficulties that had to be overcome in their construction. Amongst these feats of engineering, some especially amaze us and deserve to be called engineering marvels. Australians have created a number of engineering marvels that are still spoken about all over the world. The Overland Telegraph, constructed between 1870 and 1872, was one such engineering marvel. The huge radio telescope at Parkes, completed in 1961, is another.

COMMUNICATING WITH SIGNALS

Messages are transmitted by signals, whether they travel through cables, or as radio waves through the air. The Overland Telegraph was built to transmit short and long electric signals in the form of the dots and dashes of Morse code. Telephone cables transmit signals that are converted to sounds by the receiving phone. Pictures sent from one computer or phone to another or to televisions are also electronic signals. And the information collected by radio telescopes is received as radio signals.

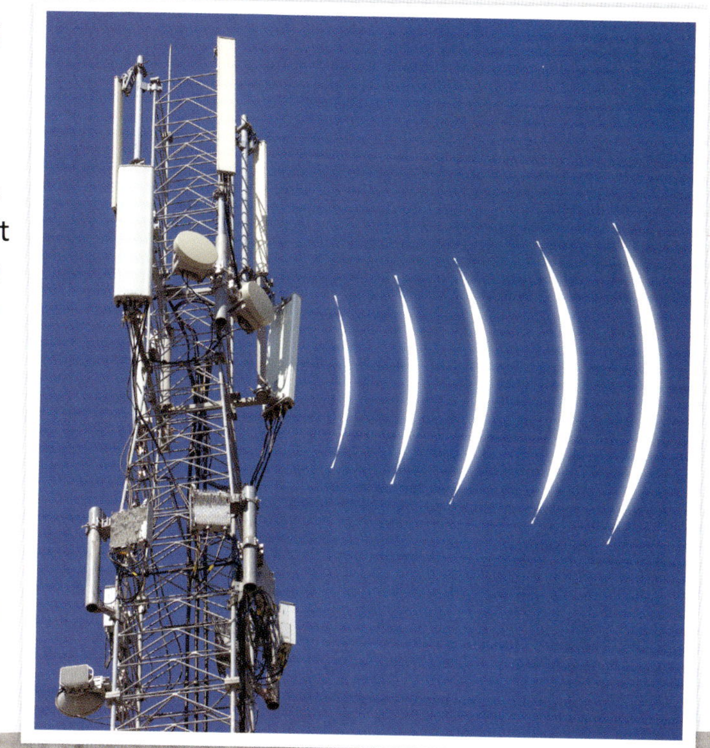

From the early technology of the Overland Telegraph, there have been many advancements in technology that have improved the speed and amount of information that can be sent and received as signals, but it is all based on the idea of signals being sent from one place to another.

The Overland Telegraph

The Overland Telegraph was a cable that stretched from Port Augusta across Australia to Darwin. It carried telegraphs, which are messages sent in the form of coded electrical pulses. Whilst today, that sounds like a very slow and low-tech way to send a message, in 1870 it was incredibly fast. The sheer distance the cable traversed made it an engineering marvel.

COMMUNICATIONS OF THE TIME

In the mid 1800s, Australia wasn't a nation, but six British colonies. Each colony was governed by Great Britain, with a governor in charge, who was appointed by the British Parliament. Communication between the governors and the British Parliament in London was limited to written messages carried by ships sailing between Britain and the colonies. These messages could take up to six months to travel in one direction. And a further six months had to pass before a reply could be delivered.

THE COMING OF THE TELEGRAPH

In 1844 an American inventor called Samuel Morse opened the world's first telegraph line between the American cities of Washington DC and Baltimore. The success of Morse's invention saw the telegraph spread all over the world.

The British Government saw the importance of linking the colonies that made up the British Empire with Britain itself. It used this new technology to set up a cable system to carry messages between Britain's far-flung colonies and London. The Australian colonies, however, were amongst the most remote in the British Empire and surrounded by sea. They were not included in the growing telegraph network.

Message Sticks

Before the introduction of the telegraph to Australia, communication between towns and cities was limited to written letters carried by coastal shipping, by stagecoach, by hand, or by messengers on horseback. Messages and responses would often take months to reach people.

Aboriginal people used a slightly faster form of communication, called message sticks. Sticks carved or painted with symbols were passed like a baton in a relay race from one place to another.

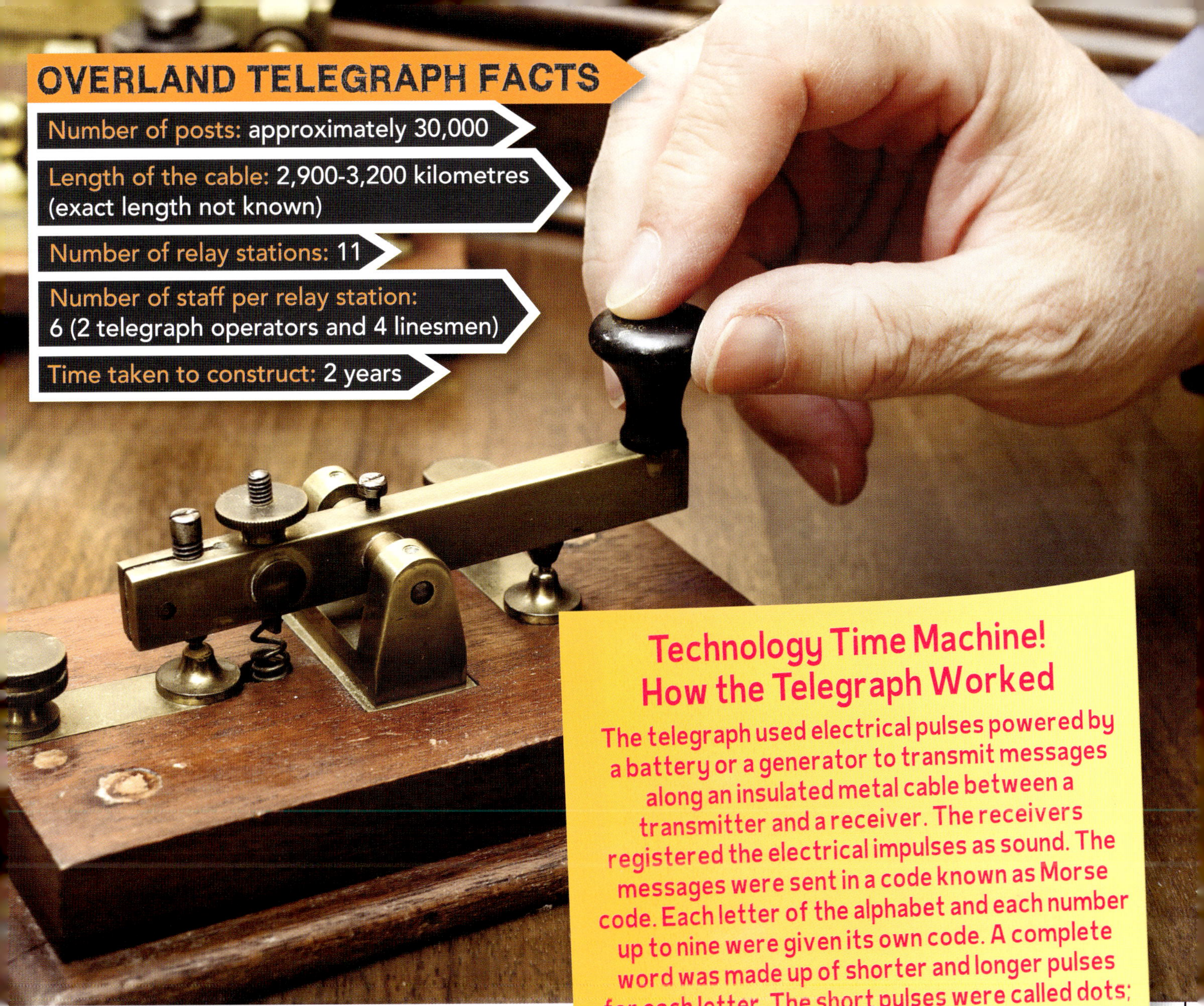

OVERLAND TELEGRAPH FACTS

- Number of posts: approximately 30,000
- Length of the cable: 2,900-3,200 kilometres (exact length not known)
- Number of relay stations: 11
- Number of staff per relay station: 6 (2 telegraph operators and 4 linesmen)
- Time taken to construct: 2 years

Technology Time Machine! How the Telegraph Worked

The telegraph used electrical pulses powered by a battery or a generator to transmit messages along an insulated metal cable between a transmitter and a receiver. The receivers registered the electrical impulses as sound. The messages were sent in a code known as Morse code. Each letter of the alphabet and each number up to nine were given its own code. A complete word was made up of shorter and longer pulses for each letter. The short pulses were called dots; the longer pulses were called dashes.

A = dot dash
B = dash dot dot dot
C = dot dot (short break) dot

UNDERWATER CABLES

Between 1854 and 1870, more and more countries joined the international telegraph network following the laying of underwater, or submarine, telegraph cables between continents. Plans were made to link the island of Java (now part of Indonesia) with Britain by means of a submarine cable. This seemed an opportunity for the Australian colonies to join the link with Britain, since Java was only 600 kilometres to the north of Australia. If the Java link were extended underwater to Darwin in northern Australia and joined to a telegraph line running to one of the cities of the Australian colonies, then communications with Britain would become much faster.

The Plan

After much debate between the colonies over which town the Overland Telegraph would run to, South Australia began work on a plan to build the cable line from Darwin to Port Augusta, a distance of 3,200 kilometres.

THE CHALLENGE

Charles Todd was appointed South Australian Superintendent of Telegraphs to take charge of the huge project. Work began in September 1870. Todd had less than a year-and-a-half to complete the Overland Telegraph so it was ready to link up with the submarine telegraph cable from Java to Darwin that was due to be ready on 31 December 1871.

Charles Todd

ARMIES OF WORKERS

Charles Todd was a man of great drive and imagination. He realised that the work schedule was so tight that one or two mistakes could ruin the project. He set up three teams of workers: one working in the far north, one in central Australia, and one working in the south. The three teams of workers would be building their sections at the one time, and would meet up. The huge amounts of materials needed to build the Overland Telegraph would all come from Britain - wire, steel posts, insulators and batteries - since Australia had few manufacturing industries to produce these things at that time. People thought that Todd was mad. The project he'd imagined was so vast, and the land that the Overland Telegraph had to cross so harsh that it was believed to be an impossible task. But Todd pressed on.

THE ENGINEERING OF THE OVERLAND

The Overland Telegraph is considered a great engineering feat because of its scale. The distance covered by the telegraph, and the difficulties of erecting steel posts and stringing thousands of kilometres of cable across desert and through flooding tropical forest and grassland, required skill and determination. But the engineering itself was simple. Posts were raised and cables were attached to them. Relay stations were built, as well as houses for the staff who would work the relay stations.

A Long, Thin Town

Electricity powers a telegraph line. In the early days of telegraphy, the electric power was provided either by batteries, or by gas and steam generators, usually fuelled by coal. Electric signals running through insulated telegraph lines grow weaker as they travel, and so it was necessary to erect relay stations at intervals to boost the power of the signals. The relay, or repeater stations had to be staffed around the clock, so the relay staff had to live along the Overland Telegraph. Houses were built for the relay staff, forming a long, thin town, with houses separated by hundreds of kilometres, from Darwin to Port Augusta.

Did You Know?

In 1942, the rest of Australia heard about the bombing of Darwin by the Japanese via the Overland Telegraph.

Construction

It took two years to construct the Overland Telegraph. This was an astonishing achievement, considering that surveying had to be carried out and that the main transport was by horseback, by camel, by foot and by bullock dray.

THE LAND AHEAD

Although the continent of Australia had been crossed from south to north by explorers, very little scientific surveying of the land had been completed by 1869. Surveyors measure the ups and downs of the land with instruments such as theodolites. Their measurements build up a picture of the shape and height of vast areas, showing where mountains, hills, plateaus and depressions are to be found.

When Charles Todd began the construction of the Overland Telegraph, he sent surveyors ahead of the working teams to reveal the shape of the land awaiting him. Because most of the Australian continent, particularly the inland, was a mystery to non-Aboriginal Australians, Todd was often surprised when the surveyors reported back. Mountain ranges, salt lakes, deep depressions, swamps and forests suddenly had to be worked into the plan.

PROBLEM SOLVING

Todd and his engineers had to invent solutions to the problems they encountered on the spot. Swamps were sometimes drained; depressions were filled in with earth and rock. Wooden posts were replaced with steel posts when white ants ate the wooden posts. When the flooding rains of the northern monsoon turned the earth to mud, Todd had to order longer posts and drive them much deeper into the ground.

Connecting the West

The colony of Western Australia joined with South Australia to build a connection with the Overland, and with the world, in 1875. The line crossed some of the driest and hottest regions in Australia, and was as difficult to construct as the Overland itself. The Western Australia link was completed in 1877, and was in use until the 1960s.

PRIMITIVE TECHNOLOGY

Most of the technology used on the Overland Telegraph was primitive, even by the standards of the time. Digging was carried out with picks, shovels and crowbars. Heavy weights were lifted using a block, tackle and pulleys. Blacksmiths, using coal forges, joined metal parts. Posts were driven into the ground by pile-drivers (which involved a heavy wooden or iron weight being dropped from a height along a shaft onto the post). The most modern technology used on the Overland was high explosive, used to clear rocks and boulders. And high explosive technology was hundreds of years old. Todd's engineers and workers were using the oldest technology around to construct the newest technology in the world.

Form No 1

TELEGRAM

No............... | Time Sent........................ | To
Time Received..

The First Telegram

On 22 August 1872, Charles Todd sent the first telegram from Australia to London. It said:

'We have, this day, within two years, completed a line of communications 2000 miles long through the very centre of Australia, until a few years ago a terra incognita believed to be a desert.'

100-AB

THE WORKERS

Carpenters, plumbers, electrical experts, engineers, sawyers, manual labourers, cooks, horse-handlers and bullockies (men who drove bullock carts and looked after the bullocks) made up most of the workforce on the Overland. At times, as many as 1000 men were employed on the project: at other times, the number of workers fell to about 200. The working conditions were nightmarish much of the time. The heat, the rain, the flies and the danger caused workers to throw down their tools and walk off into the desert on occasions. Although it is known that some workers died on the project, either in accidents or from illness, the exact number of deaths is not known.

The End

Today, all that remains of the Overland Telegraph, one of Australia's engineering marvels, is a few steel posts standing in the desert. Tourists can follow the route of the Overland, noting the rusted posts and sites of the dwellings once used by the Overland staff. Markers have been placed at significant points along the Overland route, such as at Frews Ponds in South Australia.

Bell's first telephone

OVERTAKEN BY THE TELEPHONE

Even as the Overland Telegraph was being built, work was going on that would make telegraphic communication obsolete. In the USA, Alexander Graham Bell was conducting experiments that would lead to the invention of the telephone in 1876. By 1878, Australia's first telephone service was operating in Melbourne. It would take only a few decades before much of the communication via the Overland Telegraph was being done by telephone.

Technology Time Machine! Electricity

Electrical power conveyed through power lines, which we now take for granted, was not available during the building of the Overland. Electrical power had to be generated with steam or gas turbines and dynamos, fuelled by wood or coal. The compressed steam or gas would drive the turbine of the generator, which would in turn drive a dynamo.

THE END

On 13 December 1962, the last telegraph message in New South Wales was transmitted. It was the beginning of the end for the Overland Telegraph. Telegraphic communication kept going for a few years longer, particularly in remote areas of Australia, but the end of the Overland Telegraph had been coming for a long time. By 1925, almost 80,000 Australian homes and businesses had telephones out of a total population of six million, and by 1953, one million Australian homes and businesses had telephones, out of a total population of just under nine million. Telephones were more convenient than the telegraph. People could talk to each other from the comfort of their own home. All of the information carried by the telegraph was more rapidly carried by telephone to homes, newspapers and businesses.

The Bass Strait Submarine Cable

In 1859, eleven years before the Overland Telegraph was begun, a telegraph cable was laid 350 kilometres along the seabed to link Tasmania with Victoria. Although it was only a fraction of the length of the Overland Telegraph and it transmitted telegraph signals for only three weeks, the submarine cable was an engineering marvel of its time.

A WORLDWIDE NETWORK

After the invention of the telegraph, in 1844, the first worldwide communications network began to be built. This feat required telegraphic cables to be laid over land and under the seas of the world. By 1865, thousands of kilometres of underwater (submarine) cables had been laid under oceans.

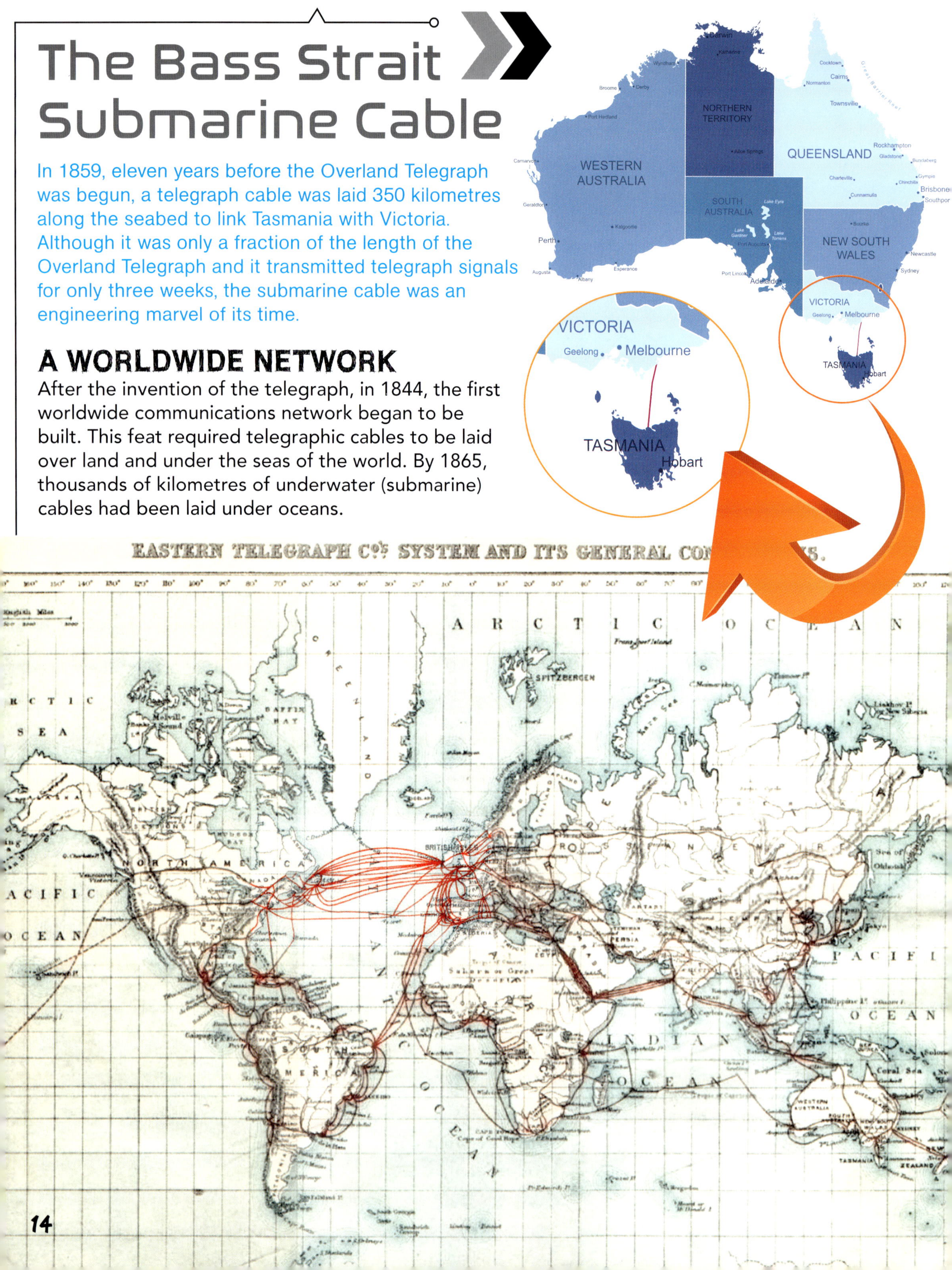

THE FIRST AUSTRALIAN SUBMARINE CABLE

In 1855, when the first plans for connecting the Australian mainland with Britain by telegraph cable were being made, the people of the colony of Tasmania were concerned that they would be left out. Even though the Java-Darwin submarine cable and the Overland Telegraph were still only a dream, Tasmania and Victoria worked together to lay Australia's first submarine cable, connecting the colony of Tasmania with the colony of Victoria. Although Tasmania was well-served by ships crossing Bass Strait carrying goods and mail, news could still take days to reach Tasmania when sent by ship.

Laying the Cable

The submarine cable was laid by ships. Enormous spools of cable were kept in a ships hold, then fed out through a special opening as the ship steamed along. The cable had to be fed out very slowly so it didn't crash too violently on the ocean floor.

THE PLAN

The Bass Strait submarine cable was to run from the tip of Cape Otway in Victoria to King Island in Bass Strait, then to Three Hummock Island, also in Bass Strait, and finally to Stanley Head near George Town on the north coast of Tasmania. The cable then joined an overland cable to Hobart.

The submarine cable would cover approximately 350 kilometres of surface distance, but because the seabed of Bass Strait was uneven, the actual length of the cable, following rises and depressions on the sea floor, was much longer. Relay stations (also called repeater stations) were to be located on King Island, where the cable would first surface, and on Three Hummock Island. It was planned that the cable would be laid in 1859. Tasmania was to become the most remote point on the globe to be served by telegraphic communication.

SUBMARINE CABLE FACTS

- **Constructed:** 1859
- **Distance:** 350 kilometres
- **Length of cable:** 500 kilometres
- **Material:** Copper wire wrapped in rubber and iron
- **Route:** Cape Otway (Victoria), Kind Island (Tasmania), Three Hummock Island (Tasmania), Stanley Head (Tasmania)

Construction

Because of the unevenness of the seabed, more than 500 kilometres of cable was needed for the Bass Strait submarine cable. In 1859, Australia had neither the factories nor the skilled workers needed to construct that length of cable.

Cross section of modern da
submarine power cable

MADE IN ENGLAND

Henley's Telegraph Works manufactured the Bass Strait cable in England. The design of the cable was the work of Charles West of the English firm of SW Silver and Company. It was Charles West who first worked out the design of submarine cables. All later designs were variations of his original design.

MAKING CABLES

A submarine cable has to be sturdy. It has to withstand the fall to the ocean floor, sometimes a drop of four kilometres. Once it strikes the ocean floor, it has to withstand the impact of the rocks on the seabed. The submarine cable was made up of layers.

At the centre of the cable were seven copper wire strands to conduct the electricity. Three coats of rubber covered the wire strands. Next came a coating of hemp stiffened with tar. Finally, iron wire was coiled around the outside. Each kilometre of the cable weighed 550 kilograms.

CABLE PROBLEMS

The first submarine telegraph cables had many problems. Although the cable manufacturers thought that the cables were strong enough to withstand anything, the first cables laid were not nearly strong enough. In 1859, when the first submarine cable across Bass Strait was laid, almost nothing was known about seabeds. Devices, such as sonographs that can create a picture of the seabed using sound waves, were not yet in use. The cable manufacturers were also unaware of the violence of the seabed. Movements of the plates of the earth's crust can cause avalanches on the seabed, and powerful currents can wrench objects about with great force.

Technology Time Machine! Copper Wire

The most important component of a submarine cable was the copper wire at its core. The copper wire carried the telegraphic signal. Copper wire was originally made by melting the copper ore to a liquid state, then letting the copper cool in long, cylindrical moulds. The lengths of copper wire were then melded together to form longer and longer strands, before being wound on spools.

The copper wire needed to be shielded from corrosion by seawater. At the time, the best material available for this job was a kind of rubber called gutta percha. The rubber would be wrapped tightly around the copper wire, or set while in a liquid state. Even this protection couldn't save the cables from being corroded by seawater over time.

TRIAL AND ERROR

It was only through repeatedly trying different kinds of cable technology that the manufacturers were eventually able to improve the cables so that they could withstand the forces of the seabed.

Laying the Cable

The Bass Strait cable was laid by the steamship Omes. Loading the huge spools of cable aboard the ship was a difficult task, and feeding the cable from the ship called for great skill. It was necessary to wait for calm weather. The cable had to be laid very slowly to prevent accidents, such as the cable snapping as it sank to the seabed. The captain, or pilot of the ship laying the cable also had to exercise great skill, keeping the ship running steadily along a straight line at a slow, constant speed.

SUCCESSFUL LAYING

The entire Bass Strait cable was laid within four months. The steamship Omes laid the cable between Cape Otway and Stanley Head without mishap. The cable was connected to a telegraph line when it crossed King Island and Three Hummock Island. At Stanley Head the cable was again connected to a telegraph line, which ran to George Town, then on to Launceston and to Hobart.

Onboard the Omes

The workers on board the Omes were skilled at laying cables and settling them on the sea floor. They knew when the cable struck an underwater hill or mountain and had to make sure the cables were paid out at the right speed to settle on them.

It was not possible for a steamship like the Omes to carry all the spools needed on the one trip. The Omes would have to return to a port at King Island and Three Hummock Island to take on more spools.

SIGNAL FAILURE

The Bass Strait submarine cable transmitted a signal from Cape Otway in Victoria to Stanley Head, and then on to Hobart, and it was thought that the project had been a success. But after three weeks, the signal failed completely. The only way to find out what had happened to the cable was to reel it in again and check its entire length for damage. The expense involved in reeling the cable back in was too much for Victoria and Tasmania to contemplate. Experience in other parts of the world showed that retrieving a cable was a very difficult business. Often, cables would snap when they became snagged on unseen obstacles on the seabed. The only solution was to lay a new cable, and that wouldn't happen for another 10 years.

Technology Time Machine! Mapping the Seabed

A technique that would have made cable-laying easier in the 19th century is echo-sounding, perfected in the 20th century. Echo-sounding, also known as sonar, builds up a picture of the seabed by bouncing sound waves off submerged objects and then measuring the time that the echo takes to return to a device on-board a ship or submarine. Sonar became important with the invention of submarines. In the 19th century, sea depths and underwater objects were detected with a rope tied to a weight that was dropped overboard and allowed to sink until the weight hit the seabed. This crude method had to be repeated every few metres, and the measurements recorded. It could be used only where the sea was shallow.

The End of Cables

The original cable, laid in 1859, lasted only three weeks. The Eastern Extension Telegraph Company laid a second cable between Flinders in Victoria and George Town in Tasmania in 1869. It lasted much longer, but it eventually failed too.

Other cables were laid each one lasting longer than the one before, but all telegraph cables became redundant as the telephone became more widespread.

Going Global

A submarine telephone cable was laid in 1893 by a French telephone company between Bundaberg in Queensland and the French island colony of New Caledonia, a distance of almost 1,500 kilometres. The cable crossed the Great Barrier Reef.

In 1902, a submarine cable was laid between Vancouver, Canada and Southport, Queensland, with a branch cable running between Norfolk Island and New Zealand. By the end of 1902, Australians were able to send telegrams to almost every country in the world.

THE ARRIVAL OF THE TELEPHONE

Once the telephone became the more popular method of communicating over long distances, the work of the cable layers began all over again. Where telegraph cables had been laid under the sea, telephone cables were laid, although over many more years than the telegraph cables. Much had been learnt from laying telegraph cables, and the telephone cables were much stronger and much more durable than those first underwater cables.

THE END OF SUBMARINE CABLES

Submarine cables are no longer laid. Satellite technology has done away with the need for them. Although telephone cables were still being laid until fairly recent times, they were far stronger than the earliest type. The synthetic submarine cables of the late 20th century could withstand almost anything, other than an earthquake.

Technology Time Machine! The First Telephones

The first telephones in Australia were awkward contraptions. The caller had to hold an earpiece in one hand to listen through while speaking into a second hand-held device. A call had to be booked through a telephone exchange. An international call might have to be booked two days in advance. The sound quality was not good and on international calls, minutes could pass between speaking into the phone and an answer coming back.

WHERE IS IT NOW?

No trace is to be found today of the first Bass Strait submarine cable - it was too perishable to survive the powerful eroding action of seawater for long. We know from underwater photography that sections of many of the cables laid under Bass Strait are still to be found, but they are now part of the debris on the seabed.

Building the Telephone Network

Today we take our telephone network for granted, but in the early days of telephones', building the network was a huge task.

THOUSANDS OF KILOMETRES

In the 1880s, when telephones first came into use, Australia was one of the most sparsely populated countries on Earth. Great distances separate Australia's six major cities of Melbourne, Sydney, Brisbane, Hobart, Perth and Adelaide. The population of Australia in 1880 was just over two million. To connect Melbourne and Sydney - the two largest cities - by telephone would mean constructing a telephone line 900 kilometres long. A Melbourne to Perth telephone line would have to stretch 3200 kilometres.

HARSH LANDSCAPE

Apart from the great distances involved in building a telephone network, there was also the harsh landscape of the continent to take into account. The building of the Overland Telegraph had shown what serious problems such a project would entail. Despite these difficulties, the creation of a transcontinental telephone network was considered a project of great importance.

THE FIRST TELEPHONE COMPANIES

In August 1880, Australia's first telephone exchange was opened in Melbourne by a private company - the Melbourne Telephone Exchange Company. It served 44 customers. The names and numbers of the customers were published in Australia's first telephone directory.

The other Australian colonies also opened exchanges:

Brisbane in October 1880

Sydney in November 1880

In 1883, exchanges were opened in Hobart, Adelaide and Launceston, each with a small number of customers

The first country telephone exchange in Australia was opened in 1882 at Maryborough in Queensland.

THE BEGINNINGS OF THE GRID

The telephone wires connecting customers to the exchanges were no more than a few kilometres in length. The first trunk line in Australia was opened in 1886, and ran for 16 kilometres between Adelaide and Port Adelaide. These wires were the start of the vast grid of telephone wires and cables that exist today.

Telephone Exchanges

A telephone exchange was a small room in which one operator sat at a switchboard and manually connected customers. As the number of customers in Australia grew, the exchanges became bigger. By the 1960s, the largest telephone exchanges, such as those in Melbourne and Sydney, employed hundreds of operators working around the clock.

Technology Time Machine! Trunk Lines

A trunk line is a telephone line that runs over a long distance and can carry a number of calls at once. They were connected to the telephone exchange. The customer would call the exchange, tell them the number they wanted to call, and the operator would connect them.

Telephone Excitement

A new telephone network and how it would work was reported in newspapers with great excitement:

'We are informed that an effort is to be made to establish a telephone exchange (in Sydney) that is, an institution which establishes telephonic communications between houses or warehouses of subscribers (customers). Then, if a subscriber at the North Shore wishes to speak to another at the Glebe, he will be able to do so by signalling the clerk at the Exchange Office, and getting him to connect the wires running to the North Shore and the Glebe residences respectively, and the conversation will go on without fear of anyone hearing it en route. This offers great convenience to business men.'

- Sydney Morning Herald, 7 August 1880

One of the World's Best

In 1901, when the six British colonies in Australia joined together to form the nation of Australia, the new Federal Government was responsible for all telecommunication in Australia. The Government set up the Post-Master General's department (PMG) to be in charge of communications.

LINKING THE CITIES

The PMG pushed ahead to build an Australia-wide telephone system. John Forrest, the first Post-Master General developed a plan to gradually link all capital cities by telephone. In 1902, the first interstate trunk line, between Mt. Gambier in South Australia and Nelson in Victoria, was opened. The line was 30 kilometres long.

John Forrest

By far the biggest engineering project of the telephone age in Australia up until that time was the building of the trunk line between Sydney and Melbourne. In 1905–1907, 900 kilometres of aboveground telephone lines were put up to link the two cities. This was followed by:

- A trunk line between Melbourne and Adelaide in 1914.
- The Sydney to Brisbane line opened in 1923.
- The 2,200 kilometre long Perth–Adelaide line opened in 1930.
- In 1936 a cable was laid under the Bass Strait linking all capital cities and some larger cities to a national telephone grid.

11 July 1907

DAILY TELEGRAPH

THE SYDNEY–MELBOURNE TELEPHONE LINE OPENS.

The telephone cable network was new and remarkable, as reported by newspapers at the time:

'The successful opening of the telephonic communication between Sydney and Melbourne yesterday affords another remarkable example of how the world is moving. There are many men in both cities who recollect the time when the transmission of a message from one capital to another was a matter of days, or perhaps weeks. It is now reduced to seconds.'

Construction crew working on telephone line in 1920

OVERCOMING PROBLEMS

The engineering problems encountered in the building of the Australian-wide telephone line and cable system were almost as difficult to overcome as those involved in the building of the Overland Telegraph. The heat of the desert, torrential rain and floods, and the dreadful working conditions endured by the manual labourers all played a part in the construction as they had in earlier projects. Despite all the hardships and all the engineering problems, the builders of the national telephone grid constructed hundreds of thousands of kilometres of line and cable, as well as servicing the grid and updating it over the years. By 1936, Australia had one of the best telephone communication networks in the world.

Technology Time Machine! Coaxial Cable

The submarine telephone cable laid under Bass Strait between Tasmania and the mainland in 1936 was at the time of its opening the longest submarine coaxial telephone cable in the world. A coaxial cable has a solid inner core of wire and an outer core of braided wires, all insulated within a waterproof coating of either rubber or plastic. Coaxial cables are much more reliable than single-core lines, and can carry a much stronger, clearer signal.

The Parkes Radio Telescope

In a field outside Parkes, in central New South Wales, stands one of Australian science's greatest accomplishments. It is a radio telescope aimed at the stars. The dish is 64 metres in diameter and at the time of its construction, it was the largest radio telescope in the world. The radio telescope of the Parkes Observatory is capable of picking up many kinds of signals from space.

MOON LANDING

In 1969, the Parkes dish played a vital role in monitoring signals from the Apollo 11 moon mission, converting the signals into pictures that were flashed around the world. The pictures showed US astronaut Neil Armstrong stepping down from the lunar landing module to take mankind's first step on the surface of the moon.

An International Effort

The creation of the Parkes radio telescope was an international effort.

Australian scientists helped build Australia's reputation as the world leader in radio astronomy.

Half the money to build it came from the USA.

Welshman, Taffy Bowen was the driving force behind the project.

Englishman, Barnes Wallis designed it.

Freeman Fox, an English company, took charge of the engineering.

German company, MAN built the structure.

The entire dish was sent to Australia in prefabricated form.

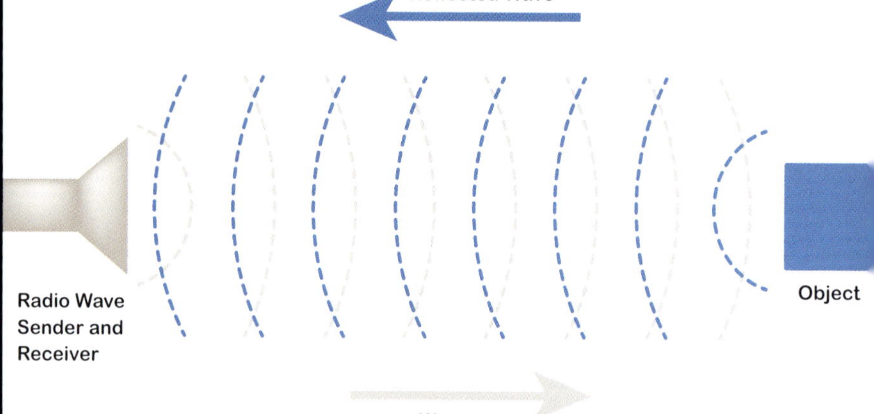

HISTORY OF AN IDEA

The Parkes radio telescope was opened for business in 1961 but the history of its construction goes back to World War II (1939-1945). During the war, experiments with radar (Radio Detecting And Ranging) led scientists to believe that it would one day be possible to pick up radio signals from all over the universe. What would be required to achieve this was a very large collecting device - a huge metal dish that would capture the radio signals from space. The signals would then be converted to electronic data. The dish apparatus would also be fitted with a powerful transmitter, so that the data could be relayed to other sites, or back to an object in space, such as a spaceship. The radio signals would allow scientists to assemble pictures of events and objects in space. This was a new means of looking at the stars - a new sort of telescope.

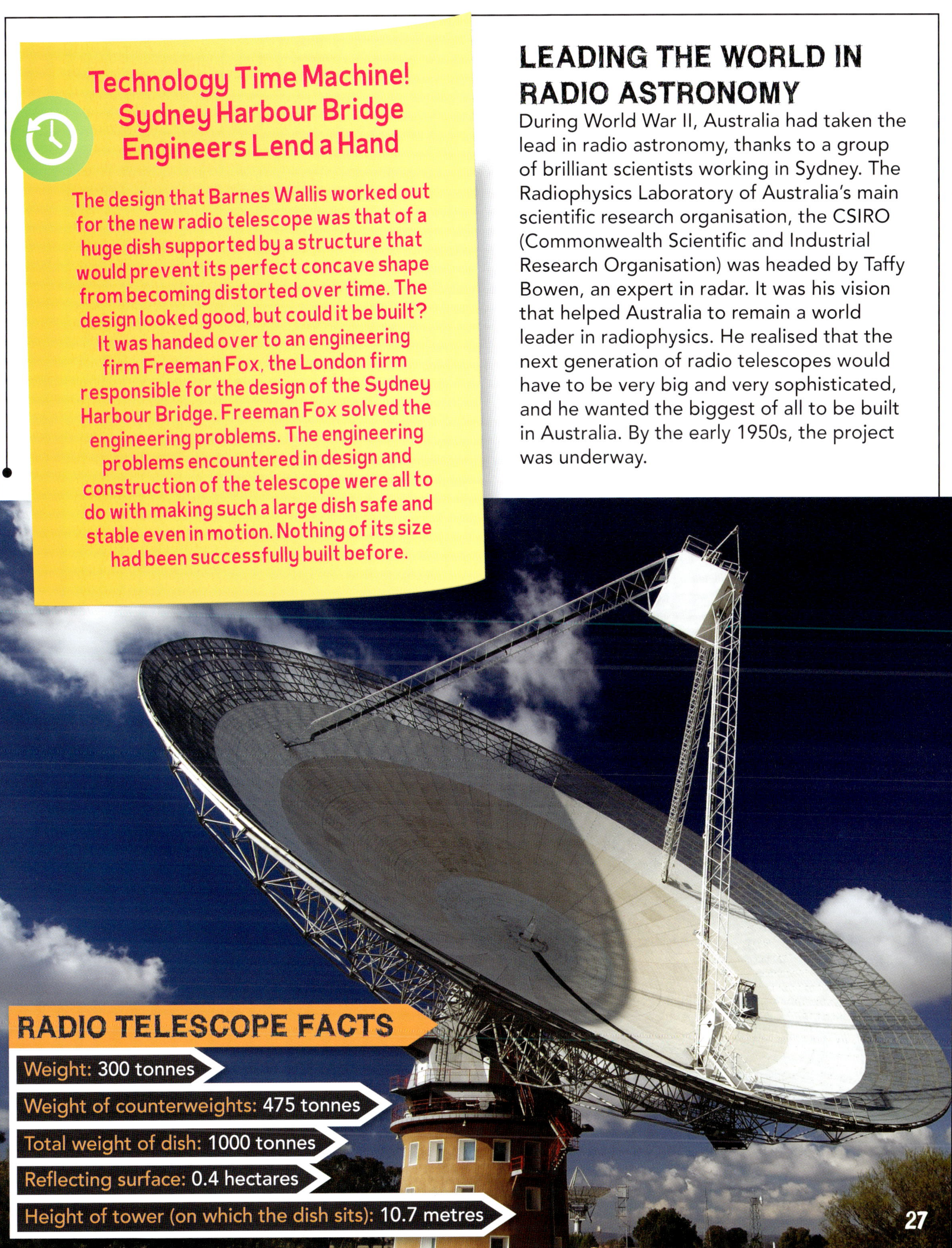

Technology Time Machine! Sydney Harbour Bridge Engineers Lend a Hand

The design that Barnes Wallis worked out for the new radio telescope was that of a huge dish supported by a structure that would prevent its perfect concave shape from becoming distorted over time. The design looked good, but could it be built? It was handed over to an engineering firm Freeman Fox, the London firm responsible for the design of the Sydney Harbour Bridge. Freeman Fox solved the engineering problems. The engineering problems encountered in design and construction of the telescope were all to do with making such a large dish safe and stable even in motion. Nothing of its size had been successfully built before.

LEADING THE WORLD IN RADIO ASTRONOMY

During World War II, Australia had taken the lead in radio astronomy, thanks to a group of brilliant scientists working in Sydney. The Radiophysics Laboratory of Australia's main scientific research organisation, the CSIRO (Commonwealth Scientific and Industrial Research Organisation) was headed by Taffy Bowen, an expert in radar. It was his vision that helped Australia to remain a world leader in radiophysics. He realised that the next generation of radio telescopes would have to be very big and very sophisticated, and he wanted the biggest of all to be built in Australia. By the early 1950s, the project was underway.

RADIO TELESCOPE FACTS

- Weight: 300 tonnes
- Weight of counterweights: 475 tonnes
- Total weight of dish: 1000 tonnes
- Reflecting surface: 0.4 hectares
- Height of tower (on which the dish sits): 10.7 metres

Building the Dish

The countryside outside the New South Wales town of Parkes was chosen as the site of the huge radio telescope because it was quiet. Noise pollution, particularly radio noise, can distort the readings. Skilled workers using prefabricated parts sent from Germany erected the Parkes dish. The structure on which the dish rests, the staff buildings and laboratories were all part of the Parkes project. It commenced in the 1950s and was completed in 1961.

A PRECISION INSTRUMENT

One of the most advanced features of the Parkes radio telescope is its ability to rotate and tilt with great precision. It can be pointed accurately at any location in the sky, and can track small objects in motion without any jolting or distortion. The dish itself weighs 300 tonnes; the counterweights that keep the dish in position weigh a further 475 tonnes. The entire dish structure weighs 1000 tonnes. The dish is rotated and tilted by electric motors and there are back-up generators in case of power failure.

Parkes Observatory

A GREAT SUCCESS

From the beginning, the Parkes dish was an outstanding success. Astronomers from all over the world have visited Australia over the 45-year life of the radio telescope to use it in space exploration and experimentation. The dish has made possible a great number of important discoveries about the nature and make-up of our galaxy and of others further afield. The Parkes dish had one of its most publicised successes in 1969, when it brought the pictures of the Apollo II astronauts on the moon to a worldwide television audience. The Parkes radio telescope regularly plays a vital role in space exploration, assisting NASA (North American Space Administration) in tracking space flights and collecting data. Over the years, the Parkes facility has become one of Australia's most popular tourist sites. Thousands of visitors each year journey to Parkes to look at the famous dish, and to tour the Visitors' Centre.

Fast Fact!

The Parkes radio telescope is continually being modernised and fitted with advanced electronic equipment.

Australian Telescope at Narrabri

THE AUSTRALIAN TELESCOPE

Since 1988, the Parkes dish has been integrated with other large Australian radio telescopes at Narrabri, 400 kilometres to the north of Parkes. The combined powers and features of the radio telescopes (known collectively as the Australian Telescope) keep Australia at the forefront of radio astronomy and radiophysics.

Cables and Signals Tourism

Learn more about these incredible engineering marvels by visiting some of these places.

SUBMARINE CABLES

While you can't visit a submarine cable without a submarine, you can learn more about this intricate world wide web of cables online. TeleGeography provides an intricate map of submarine cables at: https://www.submarinecablemap.com

PARKES OBSERVATORY

The Parkes Observatory is located just north of the town of Parkes, New South Wales. Visitors can learn about space and the universe, as well as the history of the Parkes radio telescope. There is a dedicated viewing area where visitors can watch the dish move.

LOW HEAD LIGHTHOUSE IN GEORGE TOWN, TASMANIA

The Low Head Lighthouse was the third lighthouse constructed in Australia and from 1804 was the point used to communicate shipping news from vessels in the Bass Strait. From 1859 the Bass Strait submarine cables came ashore nearby.

Glossary

block and tackle a mechanical device using ropes and pulleys to assist the lifting of heavy objects

British Empire the combined colonies of Great Britain, now known as the Commonwealth of Nations

bullock a kind of ox often used in teams to pull heavy weights

dish in radio astronomy, the large concave device that collects radio signals from space

gutta percha a kind of rubber

high explosive chemicals that produce a powerful explosion when ignited

monsoon heavy tropical rains

Morse code a system of shorter and longer sounds transmitted over a telegraph line

pile-driver a mechanical hammer used to drive poles into the earth

pulley a grooved wheel used to guide a rope or cable

radar Radio Detecting and Ranging, a device for detecting objects using radio waves

radio astronomy the study of space and of objects in space using radio waves received and transmitted by a radio telescope

radiophysics the study of the properties and uses of radio signals

radio telescope a device with a large dish and radio transmitter, used to study space and objects in space

relay station a point along a telegraph line at which the telegraphic signal is stopped and then retransmitted

repeater station another name for a relay station

satellite any object, either natural or constructed, that orbits a larger body. For example, the moon is a satellite of the Earth

sonar a way of developing a picture of a surface out of view by using sound waves

sonograph the electronic device used to transmit and receive sound waves

surveyor a person whose task it is to make an accurate recording of heights and angles in the landscape

switchboard a device used to connect incoming and outgoing telephone calls

telegram a printed form on which a typed or handwritten message is recorded after it has been transmitted in Morse Code over a telegraph line

telegraph the wires, transmission devices and receiving devices used in telegraphic communication

telephone exchange a manually operated switchboard connecting incoming and outgoing telephone calls

theodolite a surveying device mounted on a tripod and used to accurately measure angles, distances and elevations

transmitter an electronic device used to send radio signals

trunk line a telephone line connecting places a long distance apart that is capable of carrying more than one call at a time

Index

Australian Telescope 29
Bass Strait submarine cable 14-15, 16-17, 18-19, 20-21, 30
block and tackle 11
Bowen, Taffy 26-27
coaxial cable 25
colonies 6-8, 22, 24
Darwin 6-9, 14
electrical pulses 6-7
electricity 12,16
equipment 29
internet 4
King Island 15, 18
message stick communication 6
moon landing 26, 29
Morse Code 5, 7
NASA 29
Overland Telegraph 4, 5, 6-7, 8-9, 10-11, 12-13, 14, 22, 25
Parkes 4, 26-27, 28-29, 30
Port Augusta 6, 8, 9
posts 9, 10-11
radar 26
radio signals 5, 26-27
radio telescope 4, 5, 26-27, 28-29, 30
relay stations 9, 15
seabed 15, 17, 19, 21
ships 6, 15
signals 5, 14, 26-27, 30
South Australia 8, 12, 24
submarine cables 7, 14-21, 30
surveyors 10
Tasmania 14, 15, 19, 20, 25
telegrams 11, 20
telephone exchanges 21, 22, 24-25
telephone network 22-23, 24-25
telephones 12, 13, 20, 21
television 4, 5
Three Hummock Island 15, 18
trunk lines 23
underwater cables 7, 14-21

Find Out More

WEBSITES

The Overland Telegraph
http://www.australia.gov.au/about-australia/australian-story/overland-telegraph

Parkes Radio Telescope
https://www.parkes.atnf.csiro.au
https://www.csiro.au/en/Research/Facilities/ATNF/Parkes-radio-telescope